rockschool®

Piano

US Level 6 (UK Grade 6)

Performance pieces, technical exercises, supporting tests and in-depth guidance for Rockschool assessments

I0808633

All accompanying and supporting audio can be downloaded from: *www.rslawards.com/downloads*

Input the following code when prompted: **JZ3GQKL3BM**

For more information, turn to page 5

Acknowledgements

Published by Rockschool Ltd. © 2019 & 2020
Catalogue Number: RSK200095US
ISBN: 978-1-78936-171-1
Initial US Release | Errata details can be found at *www.rslawards.com/errata*

SYLLABUS
Syllabus designed and written by Jono Harrison
Syllabus Director: Tim Bennett-Hart
Syllabus consultants: Gary Sanctuary, Chris Stanbury, Simon Troup and Jennie Troup
Hit Tune arrangements by Jono Harrison and Gary Sanctuary
Supporting Tests written by Jono Harrison, Chris Stanbury, Nik Preston and Ash Preston
Syllabus advisors: Tim Bennett-Hart, Brian Ashworth, Stuart Slater, Peter Huntington, Bruce Darlington, Simon Troup and Jennie Troup

PUBLISHING
Proof reading of arrangements by Sharon Kelly, Simon Troup, Jennie Troup and Jono Harrison
Music engraving and book layout by Simon and Jennie Troup of Digital Music Art
Fact files written and edited by Abbie Thomas
Notes written by Roland Perrin
Proof reading and copy editing by Gemma Bull, Jono Harrison and Jennie Troup
Cover design by Philip Millard of Rather Nice Design
Cover photograph: © Nomad_Soul (Shutterstock)

AUDIO
Produced by Jono Harrison
Engineered by Jono Harrison, Gary Sanctuary, Tim Bennett-Hart, Pete Riley, Richard Brook, Rory Harvey and Andy Robertson
Assisted by Paul Pritchard at Abbey Road
Recorded at Dock Street Studios, The Dairy and Abbey Road
Mixed by Patrick Phillips
Mastered by Francis Gorini

Supporting Tests recorded by Chris Stanbury and Jono Harrison

MUSICIANS
Piano and Keyboards: Jono Harrison, Gary Sanctuary, Ross Stanley & Tania Ilyashova
Drums & Percussion: Pete Riley and Richard Brook
Bass & Synth Bass: Andy Robertson
Guitars: Rory Harvey, Nat Martin and Jono Harrison
Saxophone: Jonathan Griffiths
Trombone: Tom George White and Norton York
Trumpet: Nick Mead and John Simpson
Lead and Backing Vocals: Glen Harvey & Katie Hector
Additional Programming: Jono Harrison

DISTRIBUTION
Exclusive Distributors: Hal Leonard

CONTACTING ROCKSCHOOL
www.rslawards.com
Telephone: +44 (0)345 460 4747
Email: *info@rslawards.com*

EXECUTIVE PRODUCERS
John Simpson, Norton York

RSL Awarding the Contemporary Arts

Table of Contents

Introductions & Information

Rockschool Level/Grade Pieces

Technical Exercises

Supporting Tests

Additional Information

Welcome to Rockschool Piano Level/Grade 6

Welcome to Rockschool's Piano syllabus 2019. This syllabus is designed to support pianists in their progression from Debut to Level/Grade 8, through an engaging and rigorous pathway covering all the genres, stylistic elements, techniques and musical skills required for success as a contemporary pianist.

Piano Assessments
At each level/grade you have the option of taking one of two different types of assessment:

- Level/**Grade Assessment**
  A Level/Grade Assessment is a mixture of music performances, technical work and tests. You are required to prepare three pieces (two of which may be Free Choice Pieces) and the contents of the Technical Exercise section. This accounts for 75% of the assessment marks. The other 25% consists of: either a Sight Reading or an Improvisation & Interpretation test (10%), two Ear Tests (10%), and finally you will be asked five General Musicianship Questions (5%). The pass mark is 60%.

- **Performance Certificate**
  A Performance Certificate is equivalent to a Level/Grade Assessment, but in a Performance Certificate you are required to perform five pieces. A maximum of three of these can be Free Choice Pieces. Each song is marked out of 20 and the pass mark is 60%.

All elements required to participate in a Rockschool assessment can be found in the level/grade book. These are as follows:

- **Assessment Pieces**
  The 2019 syllabus comprises six 'hit tune' arrangements, benchmarked and devised so as to equip contemporary pianists with industry-relevant skills in any performance environment. These fall into three categories:

  Melody & Accompaniment
  These arrangements are performed to full band backing tracks, with the piano performing both melody and accompaniment

  Solo Piano Arrangement
  These are full solo piano arrangements, performed without backing tracks

  Vocal Accompaniment
  These arrangements cover the skills required of contemporary pianists in ensemble environments, be they on the stage or in the studio. The backing tracks feature vocalists, and the piano parts are reflective of what session pianists would perform live or on mainstream commercial recordings

  Each 'hit tune' arrangement is preceded by a Fact File, giving surrounding context to the piece and the original performers/recording artists.

  Furthermore, at the end of each arrangement you will find notes giving additional supportive context to get the most out of the pieces.

- **Technical Exercises**
  There are either three or four groups of technical exercise, depending on the level/grade:

  Debut–Level/Grade 8:
  Group A: Scales
  Group B: Arpeggios/Broken Chords
  Group C: Chord Voicings

  Levels/Grades 4–8 only:
  Group D: Technical Study

- **Supporting Tests**
  There are three types of unprepared supporting tests in the assessment:

  1. The first type can be one of two options (this is the *candidate's* choice):

     Either:
     Sight Reading tests, developing the musician's ability to read and perform previously unseen material;

     or:
     Improvisation & Interpretation tests, developing the musician's ability to develop previously unseen material in a stylistic way and perform improvised passages of melody. The book contains examples of both types of test – equivalent 'unseen' examples will be provided for the assessment

  2. **Ear Tests**
     Debut–Level/Grade 3: feature Melodic Recall and Chord Recognition
     Levels/Grades 4–8: feature Melodic Recall and Harmonic Recall

  3. **General Musicianship Questions (GMQs)**, which you will be asked by the assessor at the end of each assessment

General Information

You will find information on assessment procedures, including online assessment entry, marking schemes, information on Free Choice Pieces and improvisation requirements for each level/grade.

Audio

In addition to the level/grade book, we have also provided audio in the form of backing tracks (minus piano) and full tracks (including piano) for all 'hit tune' arrangements, technical exercises and supporting tests (where applicable). We have provided professional performance recordings of all solo piano pieces in the syllabus. This audio can be downloaded from RSL directly at *www.rslawards.com/downloads*

You will need to input this code when prompted: **JZ3GQKL3BM**

The audio files are supplied in MP3 format. Once downloaded you will be able to play them on any compatible device.

Further Information

You can find further details about Rockschool's Contemporary Piano syllabus by downloading the syllabus guide from our website: *www.rslawards.com*

All candidates should download and read the accompanying syllabus guide when using this level/grade book.

Performance and Technical Guidance

Fingering
Any fingering annotation is given as a guide only.

Interpretation
Notation should be performed exactly as written, except where there are performance indications to ad. lib, improvise, develop, etc. In these instances, the candidate will be marked on their ability to interpret the music in a stylistically appropriate way, commensurate with the level.

Adaptation
A small degree of adaptation is allowed where, for example, hand stretches do not facilitate the required notated parts. Marks may be deducted if adaptation results in over-simplification of the notation. If in doubt you can submit any adaptation enquiries to *info@rslawards.com*

Articulation & Dynamics
Where articulation and dynamics are marked on the notation, they should be followed. Where it is open to interpretation, the candidate is free to take their own approach.

Pedalling
The candidate may use the pedal freely at any level/grade, but it should be applied judiciously as marks may be deducted for any over usage resulting in an unclear tone. In addition, where pedalling is written into (or out of) the notation, this should be observed.

Chord Symbols
Most hit tune arrangements have chord symbols written above the notation. This is purely for guidance, and to assist the candidate and teacher.

Defying Gravity

SONG TITLE: DEFYING GRAVITY
ALBUM: WICKED (ORIGINAL BROADWAY CAST RECORDING)
RELEASED: 2003
LABEL: DECCA BROADWAY
GENRE: MUSICAL THEATRE
VOCALS: IDINA MENZEL
WRITTEN BY: STEPHEN SCHWARTZ
PRODUCED BY: STEPHEN SCHWARTZ
US CHART PEAK: 8

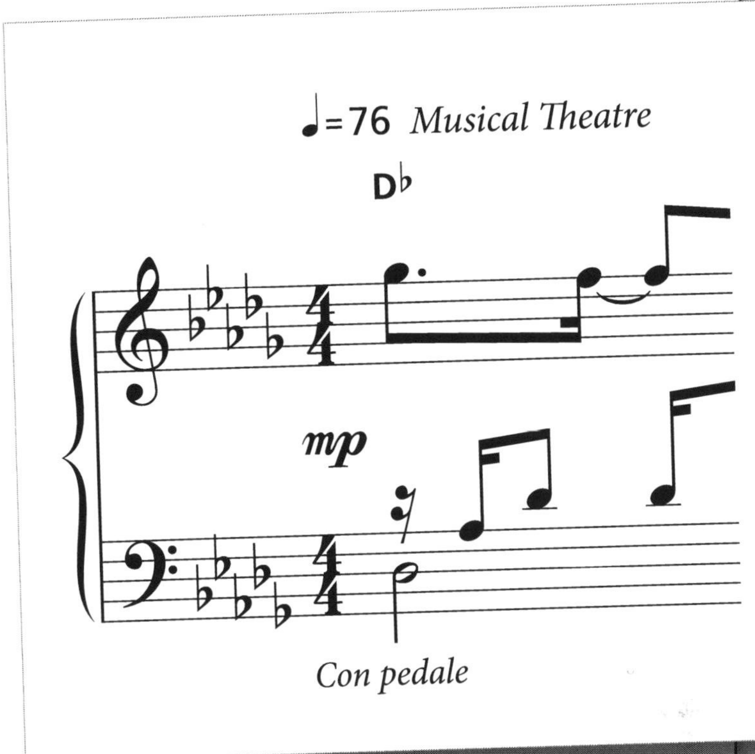

This song is the finale for the first act of the Broadway musical, *Wicked*. *Wicked* is a musical based on an alternative telling of the Wizard of Oz; from the witches' perspective. It is based on the novel *Wicked: The Life and Times of the Wicked Witch of the West* by Gregory Maguire. Apparently lyricist and composer Stephen Schwartz was on holiday when one of his friends mentioned the book. He says he was hooked immediately and upon getting home, asked his lawyer to find out who owned the rights to the book.

In 'Defying Gravity', the main character, Elphaba discovers that the *Wizard of Oz* is not all he seems and vows to do everything she can to fight him and his strange plans. During the staging of the song, the character is lifted up into the air on her broomstick, accompanied by several moving lights, smoke and wind effects. The song also incorporates two of the other prominent musical motifs from the show, to remind us of the character's journey: "unlimited" and "no one mourns the wicked". In the original story *The Wizard of Oz* by author L. Frank Baum, the Wicked Witch of the West didn't have a name. So Gregory Maguire created the name of the main character using the original author's initials: L.F.B. = el-pha-ba.

The song has twice featured in US TV show Glee – once sung by main characters Rachel Berry and Kurt Hummel, and then featured again in the 100th episode of the series as a trio, with Rachel, Kurt and also Mercedes Jones. The episode also featured Kristen Chenoweth as the character April Jones. Chenoweth played Glinda in the Broadway production of *Wicked*. The soundtrack for the musical received a Grammy in 2005 and the show itself has won three Tony awards (which recognise excellence in theatre).

'Defying Gravity' was originally recorded by Broadway stars Idina Menzel and Kristin Chenoweth in 2003. Since then many have gone on to record the hit, including Kerry Ellis, Rachel Tucker and notably the cast of Glee for whom it peaked at number 38 in the UK singles chart.

Defying Gravity

Idina Menzel and Kristin Chenoweth

From 'Wicked' (2003)

B♭m
G♭sus2
A♭
mf
[12]
B♭m
G♭sus2
A♭
[14]
B♭m
G♭sus2
A♭
[16]
D♭
G♭sus2
D♭
G♭sus2
[18]
D♭
G♭add9
D♭
G♭add9
[20]

D♭
G♭add9
D♭/F
A♭/G♭
C♭add9
[22]
C♭sus2
D♭sus4
D♭
C♭sus2
D♭sus4
D♭
[24]
E♭m7
D♭/F
G♭
A♭sus4
A♭
[26]
B♭m
G♭sus2
A♭
f expressively
[29]
B♭m
G♭sus2
A♭
[31]

B♭m
G♭sus 2
A♭
[33]
D♭
G♭sus 2
B♭m
G♭sus 2
[35]
A♭
D♭/F
G♭sus 2
[37]
A♭
B♭m
G♭sus 2
[39]
A♭
D♭
G♭sus 2
[41]
D♭
D♭/C♭
[43]

Notes

Before starting to study this piece, students would benefit from listening to the original recording to identify the different elements within the arrangement and establish a good understanding of the structure of the song.

This piece should be performed *legato* throughout. Use of the pedal may help in maintaining a smooth and balanced texture, allowing bass notes to continue to sound for their full length while allowing the performer to move hand position and play the following notes within the part. An example of this can be found in measure 1, where the opening half-note needs to sound for the full two beats while immediately moving hand position to play the following notes.

Notice that the dotted eighth-note in beat 2 of measure 1 has been beamed together with the previous 16th note. Although placed within the treble clef, this A flat should be played with the left hand. For those students with a good hand stretch, the following half-note A flat could also be played within the left hand part, allowing the right hand to play the four note descending melody. If the interval stretch of a ninth proves too much, this half note can be performed within the right-hand part, paying careful attention to ensure the separation between the melody line and accompaniment is made clear.

This arrangement contains frequent small rhythmic variations of the same phrase, in a similar way as music theatre vocalists embellish the original vocal melody – for example, compare the rhythm of the melody in measure 3 with that found in measure 5. While the pitch shape is identical, it is rhythmically quite different. It is important that students learn each phrase carefully to ensure their performance is rhythmically precise. Notice that the dotted eighth –16th note rhythmic pattern is often reversed (for example, in measure 34). The performer must avoid indavertently allowing the precisely timed 16th-note rhythms to fall into a loose triplet based swing-like rhythm.

SONG TITLE: 'AFRICA'
ALBUM: TOTO IV
RELEASED: 1982
LABEL: COLUMBIA
GENRE: SOFT ROCK/JAZZ FUSION
WRITTEN BY: DAVID PAICH/ JEFF PORCARO
PRODUCED BY: TOTO
US CHART PEAK: 1

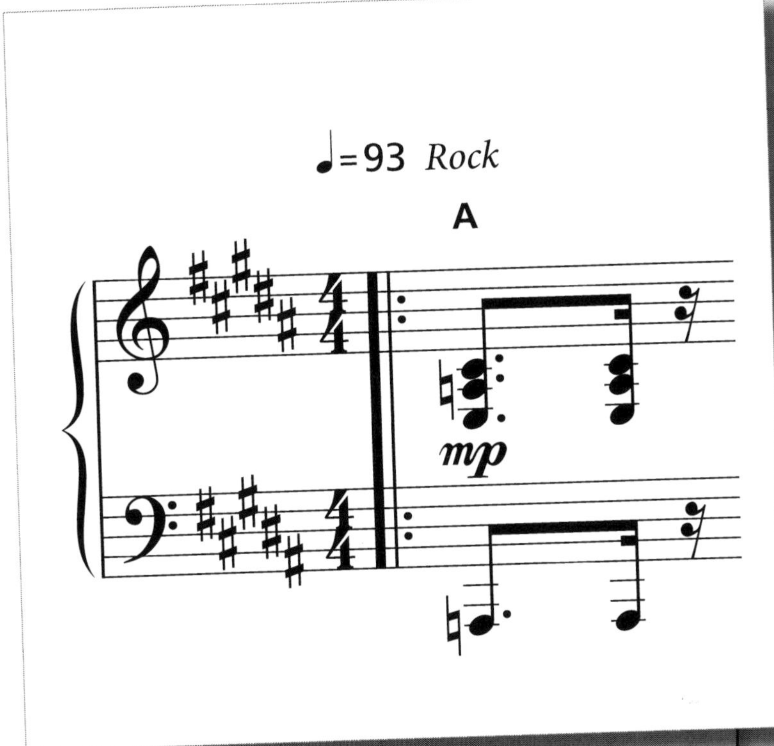

'Africa' was the third single to be released from Toto's fourth studio album, *Toto IV,* and is their most successful hit to date. Written by founding members, David Paich and Jeff Porcaro, the single topped the US Billboard chart and peaked at number 3 in the UK, making it their first US number 1 and their first UK top 5. The song also topped the charts in Canada and made it to the top ten in Australia, Austria, Belgium, Ireland, the Netherlands, New Zealand and Switzerland; making it a worldwide success.

Paich was inspired to write the song after having seen a late-night documentary about the poverty and suffering in many parts of Africa. He admits that having never been to the continent his portrayal was purely based on the media, but that he was so shocked by what he had seen that he wanted to write a song about the subject. The writing duo describe the hit as 'a man's love of a continent', detailing that the main story follows a character flying in to Africa to meet a missionary. Having attending a Catholic school, Paich met several missionaries throughout his education and was inspired by their generosity and selflessness.

The song's well recognised opening is played on a Yamaha synthesiser, with Paich using a marimba sound to create an authentic sound. The recording also features six Kalimba tracks (a traditional African instrument) all created on the same Yamaha synthesiser and playing the same rhythm but layered to create a larger sound. On recording Paich and the rest of the band worked hard to create a realistic feel, including a long percussion session which resulted in a two measure loop being chosen as the final beat. Knowing that a drum computer could have created the sound within five minutes, they took the longer option feeling that a live loop would be more effective.

In 2018 American rock band Weezer covered Toto's hit and sent 'Africa' back in to the charts. The cover gave Weezer their first Hot 100 hit since 2009 and increased popularity in Toto's original once again. Originally certified gold in 1991, the song's fame grew over the years having featured on several TV series as well as with Weezer's adaption and was re-certified 4 x Platinum in 2018.

Africa

Toto

Words & Music by Jeff Porcaro & David Paich

B
F♯m7
Dadd9
A
Eadd4
f
[13]
F♯m7
D
A
E
A/E
E
[15]
To Coda
F♯m7
D
A
Eadd4
A
[17]
F♯m7
Dadd2
A
C♯m7
[19]
E
F♯m7
E/G♯
A
Gm7
C♯m7
mp
[21]
A
Gm7 C♯m7
[23]

C
B
D♯m7
G♯m7
B/F♯
mf
[26]
A/E
E/F♯
G♯m7
A
C♯m7
[28]
B
D♯m7
G♯m7
B/F♯
[30]
D.𝄋. al Coda
A
G♯m7
C♯m7
[32]
Coda
D
F♯m7
D
A
Eadd4
[34]
F♯m7
D
A
Eadd4
[36]

F♯m7 D A Eadd4
[38]
F♯m7 Dadd2 A C♯m7
[40]
E F♯m7 E/G♯ A Gm7 C♯m7
[42]
A Gm7 C♯m7
[44]
A Gm7 C♯m7
[46]
A Gm7 C♯m7
[48]

Notes

The opening four-measure vamp requires a relaxed and laid back feel to set the initial mood of the song. The key to this passage is to establish an evenly balanced and rhythmically precise pattern. The repeated quarter-notes in the left-hand part in measures 2 and 4 require a steady and confident tempo. Students would benefit from internalising the second measure to establish a reliable quarter-note pulse before starting the perform the song.

Section A introduces the original vocal melody in the upper part of the right hand. This is sensitive music where the voice sings for the first time in the original song. The lyrics speak of a difficult choice that needs to be made. To ensure a well balanced performance, the student would benefit from spending time focusing on each hand separately to get the correct balance of the various parts within each hand before attempting to put both hands together. To secure an accurate syncopated melody line, student should isolate the upper melody line and practise along with a metronome click or counting out loud. Once mastered, they can then add in the harmony part within the right hand, paying careful attention not to allow these harmony notes obscure the melody.

Note that the final chord in measure 5, tied into measure 6, requires a large hand stretch and a fast hand position change from the previous chord. For those students with smaller hands who find this stretch too uncomfortable, try omitting the lowest note of the chord in the right hand, while making sure to play the note on beat 2 of measure 6.

There is a brief *crescendo* into measure 13, signifying the start of the chorus (section B). As the volume increases to *forte*, the music should represent the sentiment of the original defiant sounding lyrics. Students previously unfamiliar with the song will benefit from listening to the original recording to establish a good understanding of the emotional context of the lyrics and structure of the song.

Section C begins with a *mezzo forte* 16th-note solo passage, originally performed as a keyboard solo. Measures 26 to 33 contain some of the most technically challenging measures within the song and should be practised slowly with hands separately. The final performance should sound effortless, *legato* and with an even tone, keeping a steady quarter-note pulse throughout.
To achieve this, the student should establish a secure finger pattern and keep a strong quarter-note pulse to carry the music across the syncopated rhythms and time change, smoothly transitioning back into the original vamp pattern in measure 29. The music should flow seamlessly straight back into the flamboyant 16th-note solo riff in measure 30.

Students should pay particular attention to the harmonised riff in measure 30, comprising of a series of diads in thirds and fourths. Again, establishing a secure finger pattern and practising the measure as a loop at a slower tempo will help to develop a secure and confident performance.

Cantaloupe Island

SONG TITLE: 'CANTALOUPE ISLAND'
ALBUM: EMPYREAN ISLES
RELEASED: 1964
LABEL: BLUE NOTE RECORDS
GENRE: MODAL JAZZ
WRITTEN BY: HERBIE HANCOCK
PRODUCED BY: ALFRED LION
US CHART PEAK: N/A

'Cantaloupe Island' is a jazz standard written by American composer, musician and actor Herbie Hancock. Written during his early years with the Miles Davis Quintet, the piece features on his fourth studio album *Empyrean Isles* in 1964. The original recording features musicians Herbie Hancock (piano), Freddie Hubbard (cornet), Ron Carter (bass) and Tony Williams (drums).

Hancock's original composition was successfully sampled in jazz-rap group Us3's 1993 release of 'Cantaloop', featuring on their debut album *Hand on the Torch*. Although it failed to chart in the UK at first, a successful chart position of number 9 in the US led to a re-release in the band's native country where it finally charted and peaked at number 23 in the UK. 'Cantaloop' was certified gold in the US after selling more than 500 thousand copies by March 1994.

Herbie Hancock began his long and lustrous music career in the early 1960s. Having started his piano training at just 7 years old he had become an aficionado by the time Miles Davis heard him play in the early 60s. Although his training was originally classical, he found that he was influenced by his favourite artists to play and write jazz and claims that his ear taught him how to play the complex genre. His first major recognition was in 1963 when Miles Davis asked him to join his Second Great Quintet. He was a member of the official line-up for five years during which time he also managed to write and release his own solo projects, including the album featuring 'Cantaloupe Island' – *Empyrean Isles*. Having been disbanded by Davis in the official line-up, Hancock went on to feature in many of the jazz icons recordings throughout the years.

Between the years of 1962 and 2010, Herbie Hancock has released an incredible 41 studio albums. Adapting to the music industry over the decades, Hancock has successfully remained in the world of jazz for over fifty years and continues to perform and teach to this day. He is known for his diverse role in the arts, not only an extremely talented musician but also as a composer for film and television, an actor and a lecturer in Jazz. In 2016 Hancock was awarded the Grammy Lifetime Achievement Award, bringing his total Grammy wins to an impressive fourteen.

Cantaloupe Island

Herbie Hancock

C
Fm Cm7 Fm Cm7 Fm Cm7 Fm Cm7
[21]
D♭7 A♭m7 D♭7 A♭m7 D♭7 A♭m7 D♭7 A♭m7
[25]
Dadd4
[29]
Fm Cm7 Fm Cm7 Fm Cm7 Fm Cm7
[33]
D
Fm Cm7 Fm Cm7 Fm Cm7
3
[37]
Fm Cm7 D♭7 A♭m7 D♭7 A♭m7
[40]

D♭7 A♭m7 D♭7 A♭m7 Dadd4
[43]
[46]
Fm Cm7 Fm Cm7 Fm Cm7 Fm Cm7
[49]
E
Fm Cm7 Fm Cm7
[53]
Fm Cm7 Fm Cm7 D♭7 A♭m7
[55]
D♭7 A♭m7 D♭7 A♭m7 D♭7 A♭m7
[58]

Dadd4
[61]
6
6
6
Fm
Cm7
[64]
Fm
Cm7
Fm
Cm7
Fm
Cm7
[66]
F
Fm
Cm7
Fm
Cm7
Fm
Cm7
Fm
Cm7
[69]
D♭7
A♭m7
D♭7
A♭m7
D♭7
A♭m7
D♭7
A♭m7
[73]
Dadd4
Fm
[77]

Notes

This classic jazz standard is deceptively simple. It cannot be played convincingly unless the student has both consistent focus and establishes the correct relaxed groove.

The swing of the piece is dependent on a feeling of falling behind the beat without getting slower. It is essential in this regard to listen to the original Herbie Hancock recording as well as recordings by one of his major influences Horace Silver.

There is a further challenge of moving the groove accompaniment figure from one hand to the other. For example, it is in the right in the first four measures and moves to the left hand in measures 5–12. It is recommended that the student practice letter A, in a loop as follows:

- Right hand alone measures 1–4
- Left hand alone measures 5–12

It may be a useful exercise to experiment with matching the volume and attack of these passages in either hand – this will bring versatility and control to the performance.

This piece can be thought of as three distinct parts – the groove, the melody and the solo fills. There needs to be a clear difference between them. The fills should have more attack and be louder than melody. The groove accompaniment figures and bassline must be performed at a slightly lower volume to allow the melody to feature throughout. The rests in the bass line contribute to the momentum of the song (for example, in measure 1) and should be strictly observed.

The student needs to understand that the silences between the notes are vital to the groove of a bassline. As a reference, it may prove useful to listen to the work of bassist Marcus Miller.

He's A Pirate

SONG TITLE: 'HE'S A PIRATE'
ALBUM: PIRATES OF THE CARIBBEAN: THE CURSE OF THE BLACK PEARL
RELEASED: 2003
LABEL: WALT DISNEY
GENRE: ORCHESTRAL
WRITTEN BY: KLAUS BADELT/ HANS ZIMMER
PRODUCED BY: KLAUS BADELT/ HANS ZIMMER
US CHART PEAK: N/A

'He's a Pirate' was written for the opening credits of the 2003 blockbuster Pirates of the Caribbean: The Curse of the Black Pearl. Composed and produced by both Klaus Badelt and Hans Zimmer, this piece features on the film's original soundtrack which was met with mixed reviews. Despite some criticism for the album, this is arguably one of the most memorable tracks from the film score and actually charted in several countries, including top ten positions in Belgium, Finland and the Netherlands as well as a top 40 spot in Denmark.

Hans Zimmer was originally approached to write the full score for Disney's 'Pirates of the Caribbean', but given his workload at the time he decided to assign the work to his colleague Klaus Badelt. Despite having delegated the work out to a fellow composer, Zimmer still became heavily involved and actually ended up writing most of the score himself. Zimmer is well known for his work on box office hits such as The Lion King, Gladiator, Inception, The Dark Knight Trilogy and of course The Pirates of the Caribbean series.

Zimmer's music career started in the UK, where he spent some time playing keyboard and synthesizers for various bands in the 1970s. He actually makes an appearance in the Buggles' music video for their hit 'Video Killed the Radio Star'.

The composer launched his career as a film scorer by first writing jingles for Air Edel, a world leading music production company. From here, he went on to join forces with prolific film composer Stanley Myers with whom he co-founded Lillie Yard recording studio. It was with Myers that Zimmer first used his now identifiable technique of blending orchestral music with electronic sound. In 1988 Zimmer was approached by a Hollywood director requesting that he write the score for his up and coming release, 'Rain Man'. Zimmer accepted and made the move to Hollywood, where he is now the head of the film music division at DreamWorks Studios.

Although his work on the 'Pirates of the Caribbean' soundtrack was met with mixed reviews and failed to win him any awards, Zimmer has in the past been highly regarded in the world of film scoring and has won several awards. In 1995 his score for The Lion King won the Academy Award for Best Original Score as well as a Golden Globe and two Grammys that same year.

He's A Pirate

Klaus Badelt, Geoffrey Zanelli and Hans Zimmer

From 'Pirates of the Caribbean: The Curse of the Black Pearl' (2003)

[11]
[13]
[15]
[17]
8vb
[19]

[21]
f
8vb
[23]
[25]
[27]
mf
5 2 1 2
Ped.
[29]
[31]

[33]
[35]
f
[37]
Ped.
[39]
Ped.
[41]
[43]
fp
Ped.
8vb

Notes

Students should aim for a feeling of perpetual motion all the way through this piece. It is important that the notes are learnt slowly, the two hands separately at first, paying particular attention to the correct fingering.

Students should be careful not to change the articulation during the *crescendo* in the first four measures. Every note should be *staccato*, and exactly the same length. Aim for a controlled and evenly developed *crescendo*, avoiding raising the volume too quickly.

The overall shape of the song must be kept in mind. The first climax is at measure 21. Note the changing use of articulation in the left hand part of measures 21 to 23. Students might benefit from practising the part in isolation and as a loop to ensure a clear distinction between the *staccato* and *non-staccato* notes. Once secure, students should practise fitting both parts together. If this is proving challenging, try practising with an eighth-note foot tap, or along to a metronome click at a much slower tempo. This passage should sound confident and full of energy and drive. However, there is potential to speed up throughout this passage and students will need to keep a brisk but steady internal pulse throughout.

From the upbeat into measure 28, there is an immediate change of mood, requiring *legato* lyrical lines and a sweeping bass line pattern. Precise pedalling is very important in this passage to avoid loss of clarity.

The storm is unleashed again in measure 36, where the dynamic level returns to *forte*. This is emphasised by the crashing accented chords in measures 37 and 43. Student must make sure they play these measures without the pedal for accurate observation of the rests, adding drama to the moment.

The final *tremolando* on the octave 'D's starts loudly, and then must immediately drop to *piano* as the storm dies away.

In The End

SONG TITLE: 'IN THE END'
ALBUM: HYBRID THEORY
RELEASED: 2001
LABEL: WARNER BROS.
GENRE: NU METAL/RAP ROCK
WRITTEN BY: BRAD DELSON/ CHESTER BENNINGTON/ JOE HAHN/ MIKE SHINODA/ ROB BOURDON
PRODUCED BY: DON GILMORE
US CHART PEAK: 2

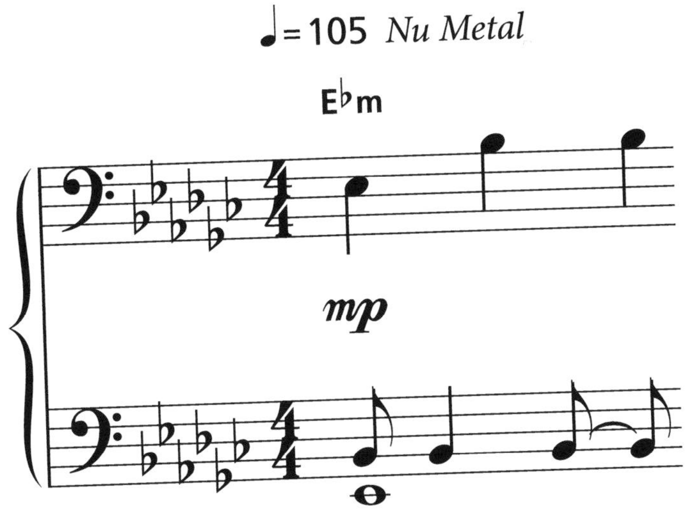

'In the End' was the fourth single to be released from nu metal band Linkin Park's debut album, *Hybrid Theory.* Although lead singer Chester Bennington originally wanted to drop the song the band managed to persuade him that it should be included in their release, a decision which proved fruitful as the song made it to the top ten in several countries and number 2 in the US. The song made it to number 8 on the UK singles chart, making it their highest charting release since their debut with 'One Step Closer'.

'In the End' was written by the founding members of Linkin Park; Brad Delson, Chester Bennington, Joe Hahn, Mike Shinoda and Rob Bourdon. Since it's release, the track has been held in high regard and is thought of by many as one of the greatest nu metal hits of the 00s. Not only did VH1 rate it 84th on the list of their 100 Greatest Songs of the 00s, but Loudwire Magazine ranked it number 2 on their list of 'Top 21st Century Hard Rock Songs'. Linkin Park do well to take this feedback on and the hit remains their second most performed live song to date.

Linkin Park formed in 1996, with three of the members having been high school friends in Agoura Hills California. The three friends, Bennington, Shinoda and Delson, went on to enroll the help of Joe Hahn, Dave Farrell and Wakefield to join their then named band Xero. The young band had very little in the way of resources, but this didn't hold them back and they succeeded in recording their first demo EP in Shinoda's makeshift bedroom studio. Frustrated with the lack of immediate recognition, both Wakefield and Farrell decided to leave the band and move on to other projects.

After much hard work, the band finally signed their first major label deal with Warner Bros. in 1999 and went on to release their debut album *Hybrid Theory.* No one could have guessed its success, with sales in its first year exceeding 4.8 million copies and making it the best-selling album of 2001. Following a successful career launch, Linkin Park went on to release seven studio albums of which 3 made it to number 1 in the UK album charts.

Frontman Chester Bennington struggled with depression for much of his life and sadly lost his battle with the illness in 2017. Linkin Park continue to tour in his memory and he will remain an influential figure in the world of nu metal for years to come.

In The End

Linkin Park

Words & Music by Chester Bennington, Mike Shinoda, Rob Bourdon, Joseph Hahn & Brad Delson

D♭sus2
E♭madd9
D♭6
[16]
C♭maj7♯11
D♭sus2
E♭madd9
[19]
D♭6
C♭maj7♯11
D♭sus2
[22]
B
E♭madd9
G♭
D♭
f
[25]
C♭
E♭madd9
G♭
[28]

D♭
C♭
[31]
C
E♭m
D♭
C♭maj7
p
[34]
D♭
E♭m
D♭
[37]
C♭maj7
D♭
E♭m add9
f
[40]
G♭
D♭
C♭
[43]

E♭madd9
G♭
D♭
[46]
D
C♭
E♭madd9
G♭
ff
[49]
D♭
C♭
E♭madd9
[52]
G♭
D♭
C♭
[55]
E
E♭m
mp
[58]
rit.
E♭madd9
[61]

Notes

The opening eight-measure introduction requires a steady tempo and careful phrasing. Note the three part texture and the different roles each element plays. While these measures might look deceptively straightforward, they require a considered and thoughtful approach to allow each part to work together, balanced appropriately. The pared down melody with repeated notes and constant quarter-note movement needs subtle phrasing to set the emotional context of the song. Equally important is the insistent, repetitive syncopated middle part helping to keep the momentum of the music. Be careful not to allow this to become overstated or rise above the right-hand melody. Students would benefit from listening to an original recording of the song to develop a good understanding of the character of the piece.

Section A requires a smooth *legato* left hand accompaniment, which continues through much of the song. Here it is recommended that slow practise is done with the left hand alone, ensuring that every note is of equal volume. The student should attempt this before any sustain pedal is introduced. A relaxed wrist and gently rounded finger position will help faciliate an even tone as the hand moves position through the arpeggios. However, strength and consistency of tone is just as important as a light hand and regular practise of both scales and arpeggios will help build up finger strength, enabling better control over *legato* passages.

Students should observe the dynamics to help shape and structure the song. Note that the *crescendo* in measures 16 to measure 25 will require careful control to allow for a very gradual increase in volume that both avoids peaking too early and only rises to a final *forte*. This slow and insistent increase in volume will help add to the sense of building drama. The performer must keep some volume in reserve to be able to provide further contrast later in the piece where the music peaks in measure 50 (start of section D).

There also needs to be full understanding of when the change of mood is not the result of a slow and controlled *crescendo*, or subtle *diminuendo* (measures 57 to 59) but requires a sudden change (for example, in measure 41). Accurate observance of each of these different shifts in volume will help to create a convincing and emotionally charged performance.

The Way It Is

SONG TITLE: THE WAY IT IS
ALBUM: THE WAY IT IS
RELEASED: 1986
LABEL: RCA
GENRE: SOFT ROCK
VOCALS: BRUCE HORNSBY
PIANO: BRUCE HORNSBY
GUITAR: DAVID MANSFIELD
BASS: JOE PUERTA
DRUMS: JOHN MOLO
WRITTEN BY: BRUCE HORNSBY
PRODUCED BY: BRUCE HORNSBY, ELLIOT SCHEINER
US CHART PEAK: 1

'The Way it Is' was written by Bruce Hornsby and focuses on the American Civil Rights Movement. The lyrics specifically mention the Civil Rights Act of 1964, stating: "well they passed a law in '64". The law was intended to ban any kind of discrimination in public places and employment, but of course terrible amounts of discrimination still existed in US at the time of Hornsby's single release. His lyrics are literally telling the listener not to accept 'the way it is'.

Bruce Hornsby had worked as a 'staff songwriter' and session musician for several years, but due to his preference for blending different types of jazz sounds he hadn't had any mainstream success. He says: "I could have easily sacked it in, but I stayed intense. I still am." He created a demo, nevertheless, which was eventually picked up by major label RCA who, he said, offered him the creative freedom he was looking for.

Hornsby studied music at three universities, including Berklee College of Music, before graduating from the University of Miami. On graduating, he formed a songwriting duo with his brother, John, and they spent three years writing for Twentieth Century Fox. He credits his dedication to sport (he plays basketball) for giving him the discipline and staying-power to succeed in his musical career. Hornsby is also credited as a talented piano improviser and has won three Grammy awards.

He has collaborated with the Grateful Dead, playing over 100 shows with them. Grateful Dead are famed for their eclectic style, featuring: Bluegrass, Improvised Jazz, Psychedelia and instrumental jams.

The song was heavily sampled in 1998 by rapper Tupac Shakur in his song 'Changes', which looks at racism, the war on drugs and the behavior of the US police towards black people at the time.

The Way It Is

Bruce Hornsby and the Range

Words & Music by Bruce Hornsby

Am7 Em7 D Cadd9 G D Cadd9
[17]
B
Am7 Em7 D Cadd9 G D Cadd9
[21]
Am7 Em7 D Cadd9 G D Cadd9
[25]
Gadd9 Fmaj7 C Gadd9 Fmaj7 C
[29]
Gadd9 Fmaj7 C
To Coda
[32]
Gadd9 Fmaj7 C Am7 Em7
[35]

1.
2.
D
Cadd9
G
D
Cadd9
Cadd9
[38]
C
Am
Em
D
C
G
D
C
[42]
Am
Em
D
C
G
D
[46]
C
Am
Em
D
C
[49]
G
D
C
Am
Em
[52]
D
C
G
D
C
[55]

Am Em D C G D C
[58]
Gadd9 Fmaj7 C Gadd9 Fmaj7 C
D.S. al Coda
[62]
Coda
Gadd9 Fmaj7 C
[66]
D
Am7 Em7 D C G D
[68]
C Am7 Em7
[71]
D C G D
[73]

C
Am7
Em7
[75]
D
C
G
D
[77]
C
Am7
Em7
[79]
D
Cadd9
G
D
Cadd9
[81]
Gadd9
Fmaj7
C
8
Gadd9
Fmaj7
C
[84]
Gadd9
Fmaj7
C
[87]

Gadd9
Fmaj7
C
[89]
[92]
[95]
E
[98]
[100]
Repeat ad lib. to fade

Notes

To understand the significant role that the piano played in the original version of this song, students should listen to the original recording before starting to learn the notes.

The right-hand part in the opening eight measures require the performer to allow the melody to ring out while playing the inner accompaniment part within the same hand. Students would benefit from playing the right hand in isolation, first playing only the melody notes, before adding in the accompaniment embellishments, taking care that the melody is still very clearly heard above (for example, in measure 2). Note the chord voicing in the bass clef in measure 4 creates an interval of a tenth. While some students might be able to play this comfortably, for students with smaller hands, play the upper note (E) with the right hand, allowing the pedal to assist in allowing the chord to continue sounding through the measure while moving hand position to play the following notes.

At the start of section A, there is a noticeable change in tempo. Be careful to observe the rests in measure 12 to allow for a precise and clear 16th-note *legato* phrase played with the left hand.

Students should notice the use of grace notes as embellishments throughout the piece. These should be precisely timed to allow the main notes fall on the beat and not affect the steady pulse within the measure.

The rhythmic pattern found in the right hand part of measure 29 returns throughout the song. Be careful not to rush the 16th notes, playing this important motif precisely in time. Measures 29 to 36 are worth learning in isolation, initially only playing the right-hand part along with a clear eighth-note count or tap and at a slower tempo. When secure, introduce the accompanying syncopated bass line in the left hand, while keeping a strong internal pulse throughout.

As much of the arrangement uses material that was originally written for the piano, the majority of the 16th-note passages found in the right hand part within sections C and D fit comfortably under the fingers. However, students should establish secure finger patterns and practise each passage at a slower tempo to ensure a *legato* and effortless sounding performance.

The rhythm pattern in measures 58 to 61 may prove challenging for students. Try playing these four measures slowly, temporarily changing the rhythm of the left hand part to quarter notes to help understand where the notes fall across the beat. Once secure, the performer can return to the correct half-note movement while keeping a steady internal quarter-note pulse.

The final repeated four measures of the song (section E) should to be performed with clear focus on articulation. Students should know which notes are to be played *staccato* and which are to be played for their full duration. Time spent playing these four final measures at a slower tempo to master the synopcated rhythmic patterns and correct articulation will help to prepare for a confident and precise final performance.

Technical Exercises

In this section you will be required to play a selection of exercises drawn from each of the groups below. The assessor will be looking for the speed of your response and will also give credit for the level of your musicality. Please see the syllabus guide for details on the marking criteria.

- Candidates must prepare ***both*** natural minor ***and*** harmonic minor scales
- Major scales, minor scales, chromatic scales and arpeggios need to be played hands together, in straight or swung feel, ascending and descending, across ***four*** octaves (except contrary motion scales, pentatonics, lydian dominant and locrian modes, which must be played over ***two*** octaves, and extended arpeggios which are ***one*** octave only)
- Groups A, B and C (scales, arpeggios and chords) need to be played from memory. You may use your book for Group D (technical studies)

Note that Groups A and B need to be played to a click and any fingerings shown are suggestions only.

Group A: Scales
The tempo for this group is ♩=152 bpm.

1. F♯ major *(four octaves, two octave example shown)*

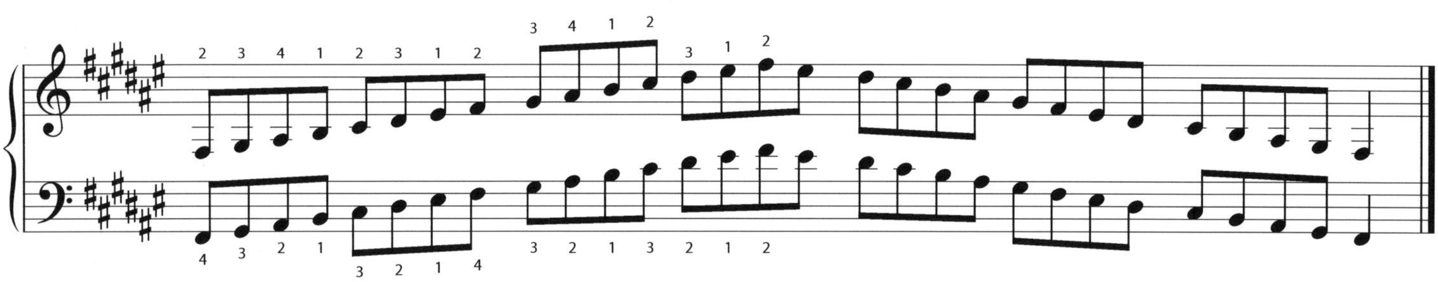

2. F♯ major | contrary motion

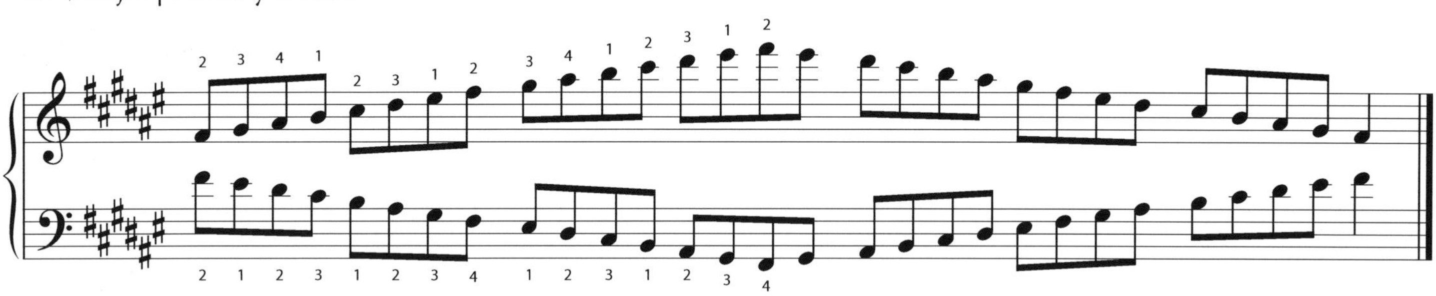

3. G♭ major *(four octaves, two octave example shown)*

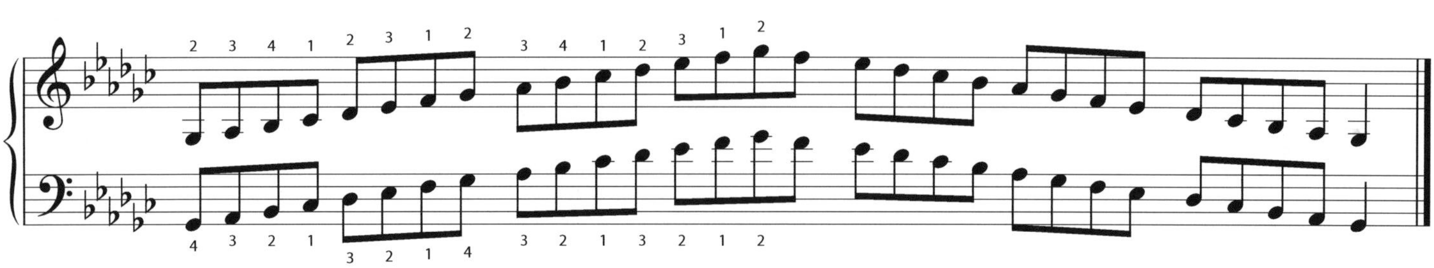

4. G♭ major | contrary motion

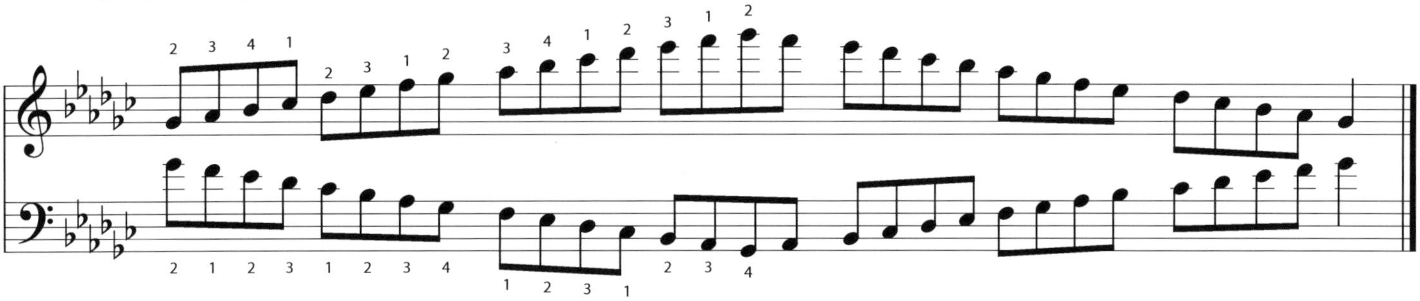

5. D♯ natural minor *(four octaves, two octave example shown)*

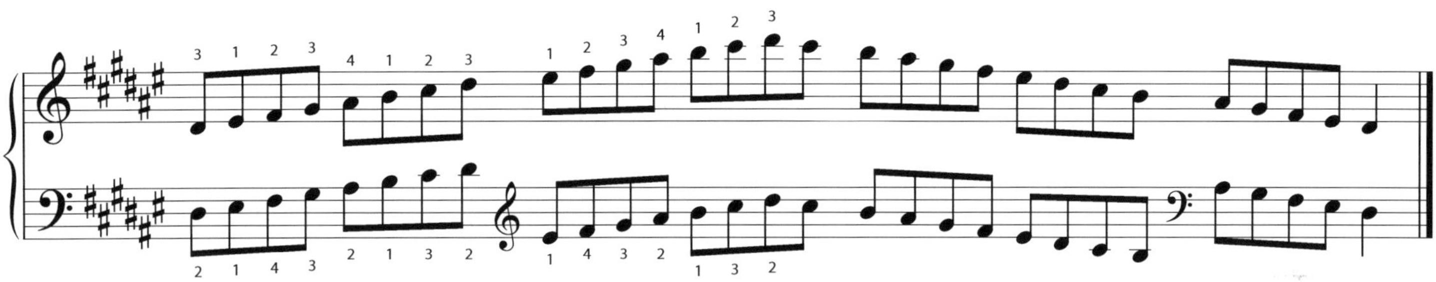

6. E♭ natural minor *(four octaves, two octave example shown)*

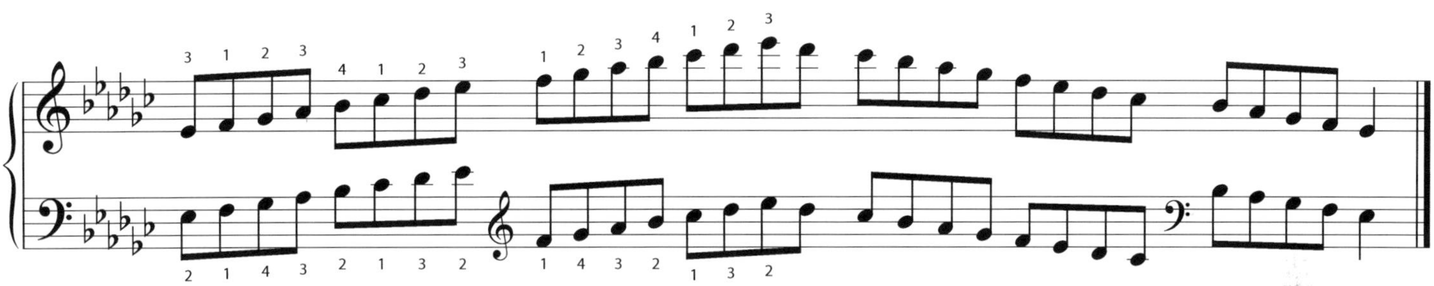

7. D♯ harmonic minor *(four octaves, two octave example shown)*

8. E♭ harmonic minor *(four octaves, two octave example shown)*

9. F♯ major pentatonic

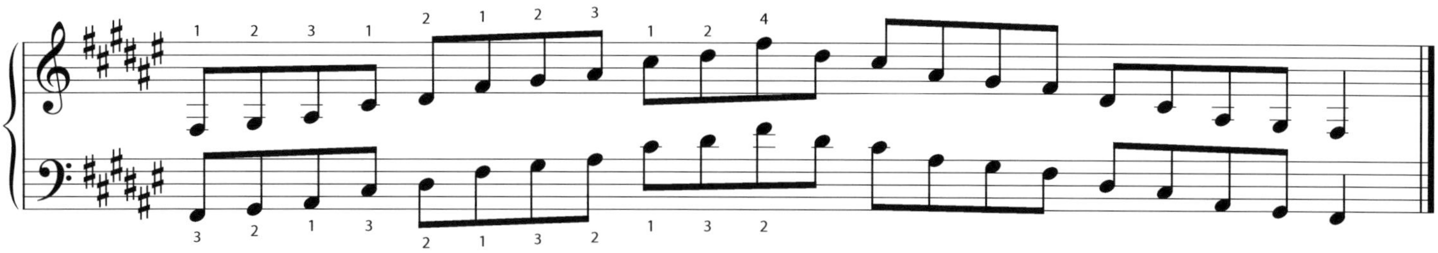

10. G♭ major pentatonic

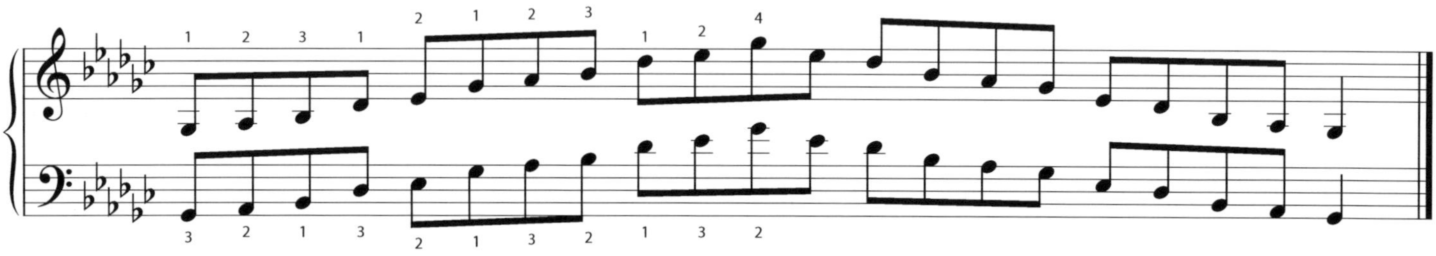

11. D♯ minor pentatonic

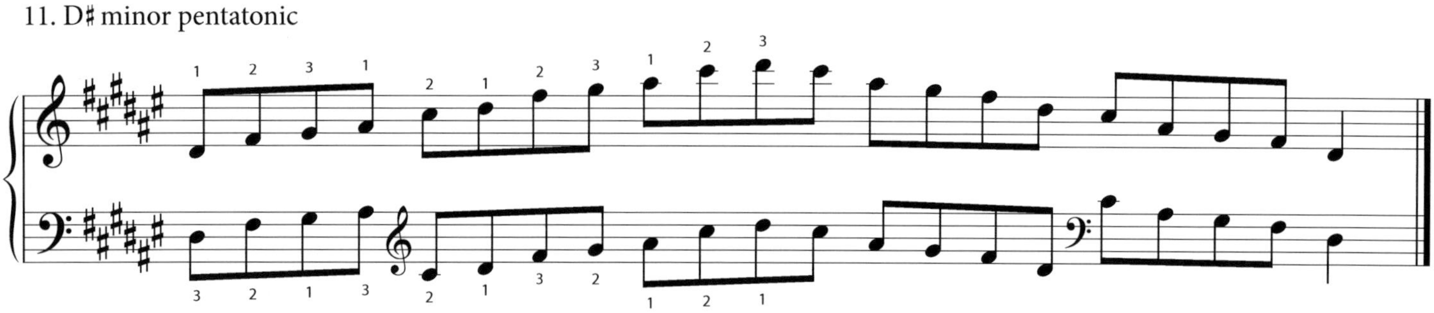

12. E♭ minor pentatonic

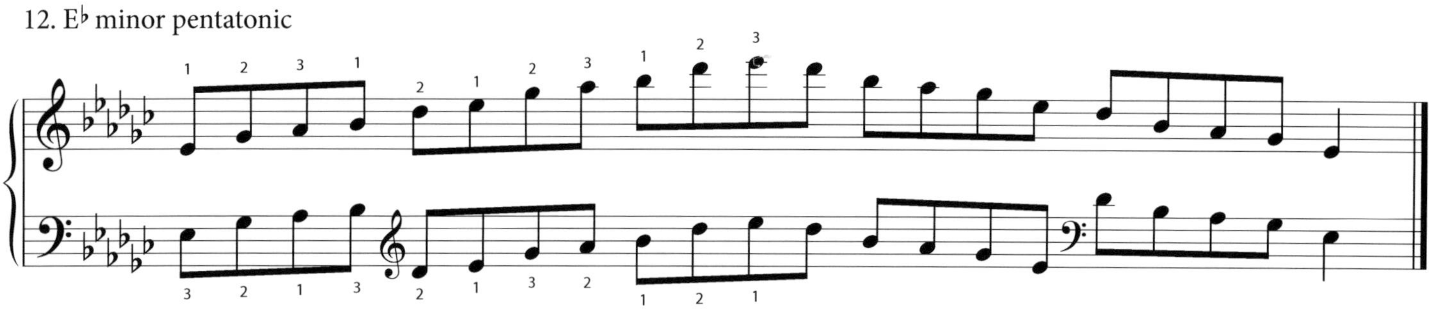

13. C lydian dominant

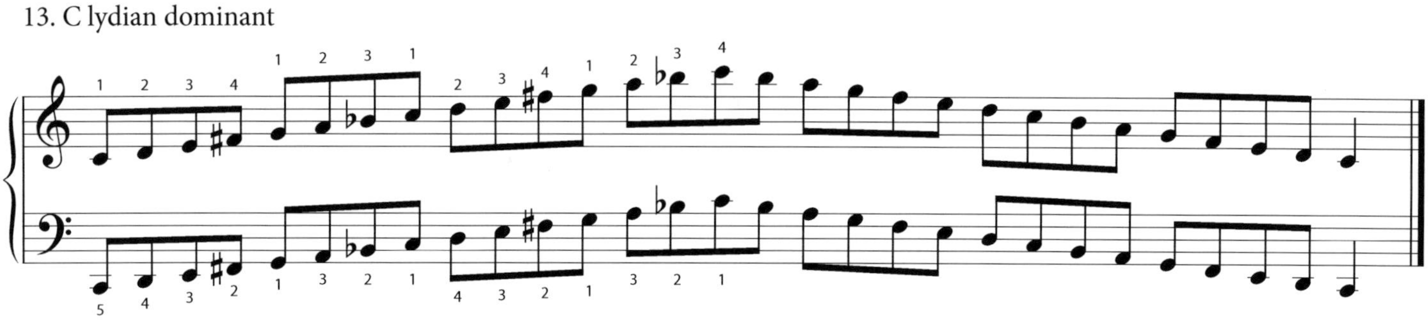

14. C locrian

15. Chromatic scale | starting on any black key stated by assessor, example given in F♯ *(four octaves, two octave example shown)*

Group B: Arpeggios

The tempo for this group is ♩=100 bpm.

1. F♯ major arpeggio *(four octaves, two octave example shown)*

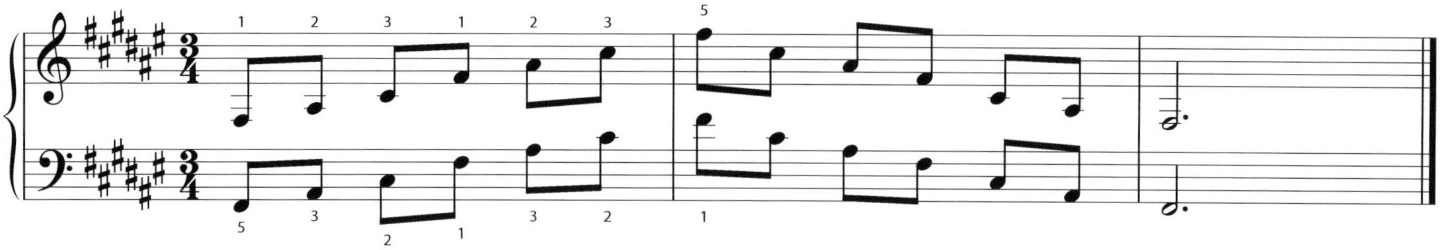

2. G♭ major arpeggio *(four octaves, two octave example shown)*

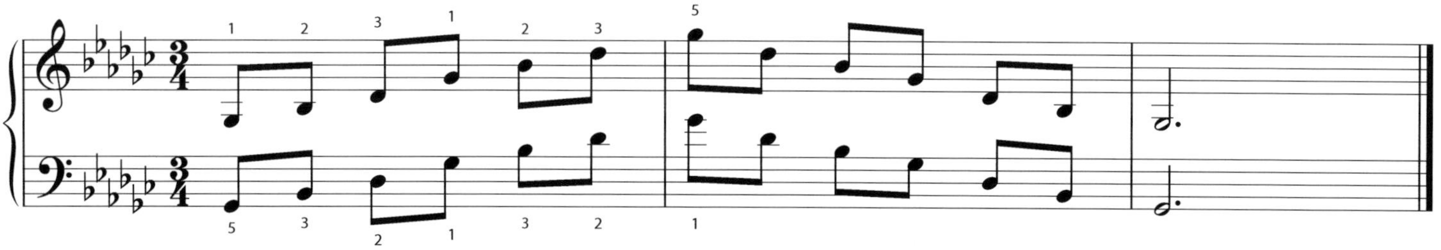

3. D♯ minor arpeggio *(four octaves, two octave example shown)*

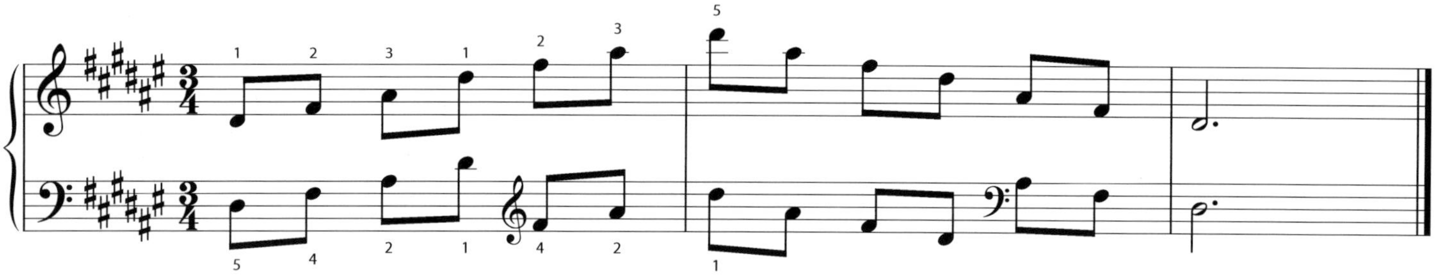

4. E♭ minor arpeggio *(four octaves, two octave example shown)*

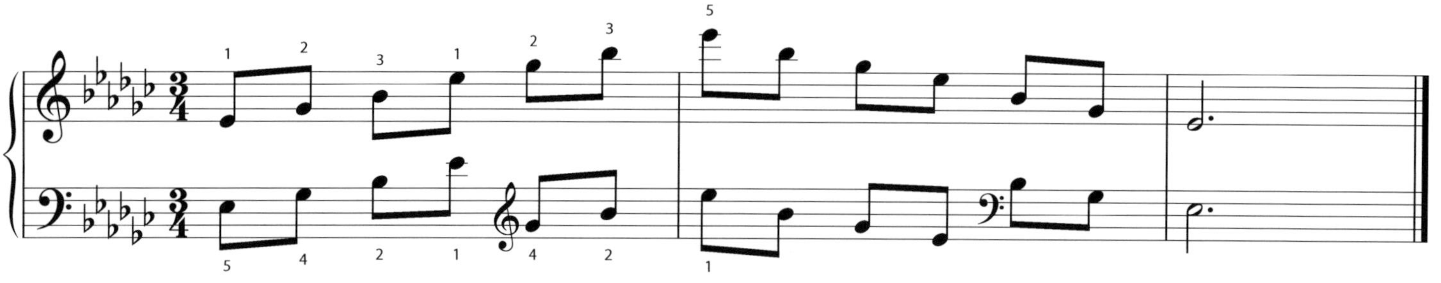

5. G^7 arpeggio *(four octaves, two octave example shown)*

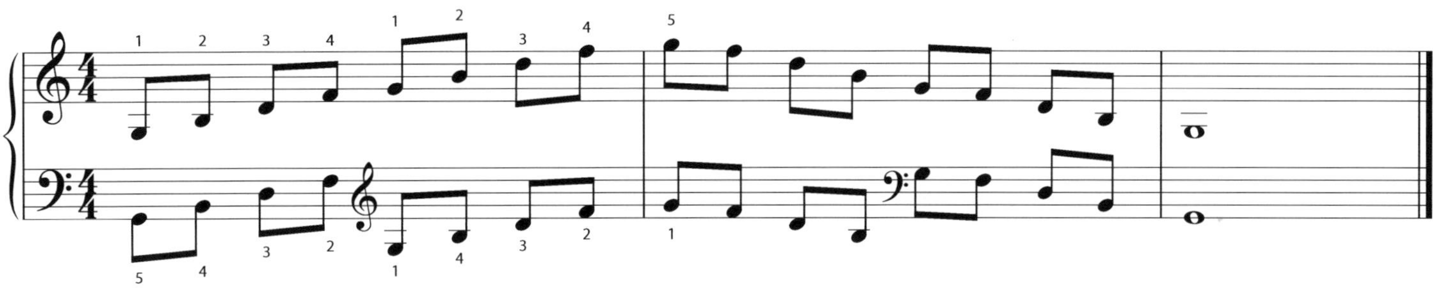

6. F^7 arpeggio *(four octaves, two octave example shown)*

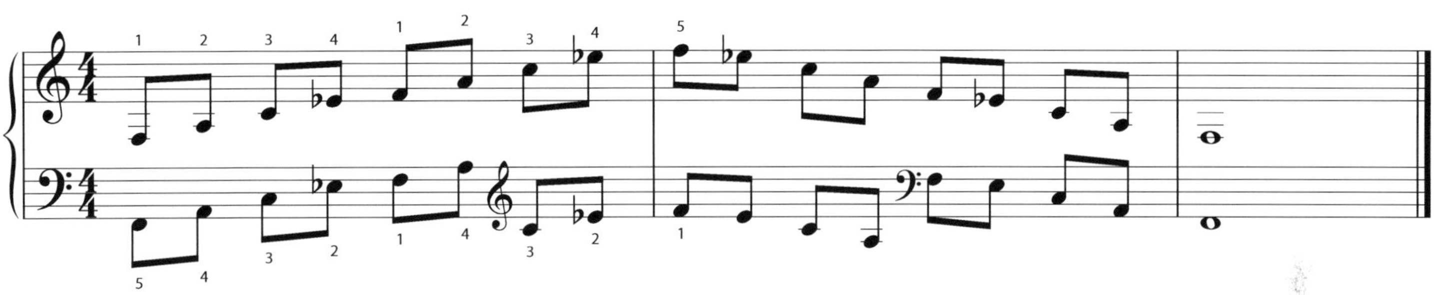

7. C♯dim^7 arpeggio *(four octaves, two octave example shown)*

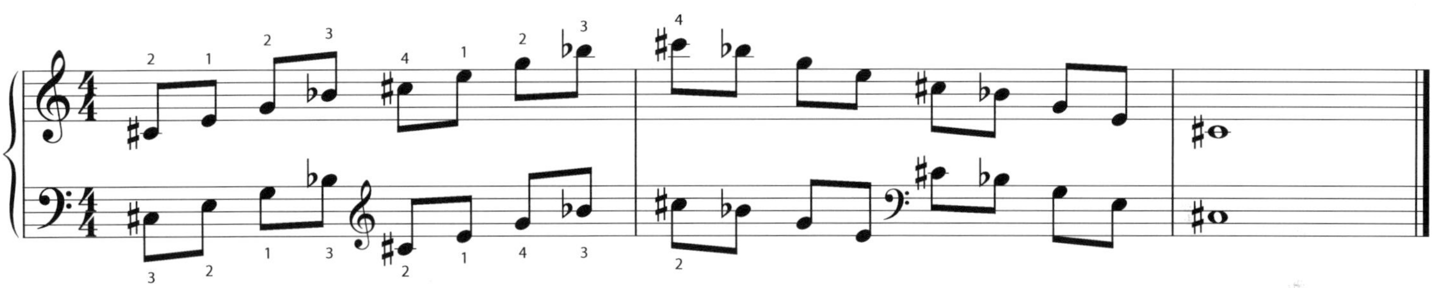

8. C$^{13\sharp11}$ arpeggio

9. C$^{7\sharp5\sharp9}$ arpeggio

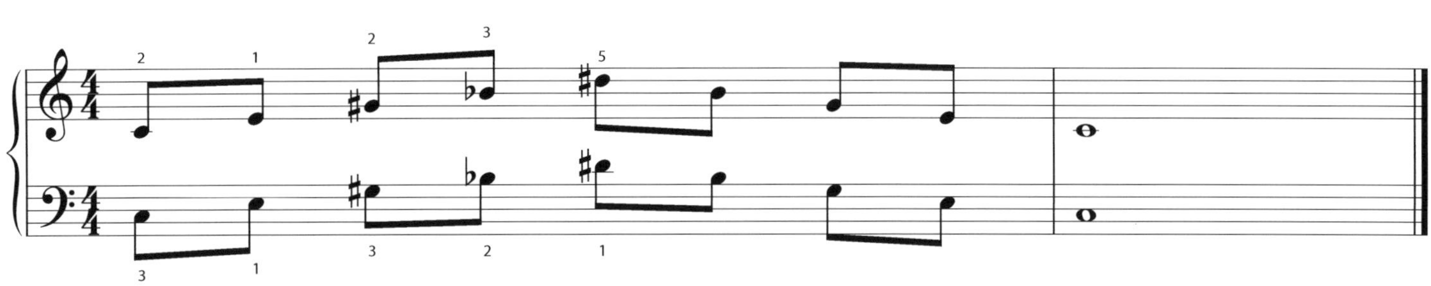

Group C: Chord Voicings | Major ^{13}, Dominant ^{13} and Minor ^{13} Chords

In the assessment you will be asked to play *one of the* chord exercises below, from memory. The assessor will state the chord type. This test is performed in free time (without backing track or click), but the assessor will be looking for the speed of your response.

Ex 1: Cmaj^{13} chords

Ex 2: C^{13} chords

Ex 3: Cm^{13} chords

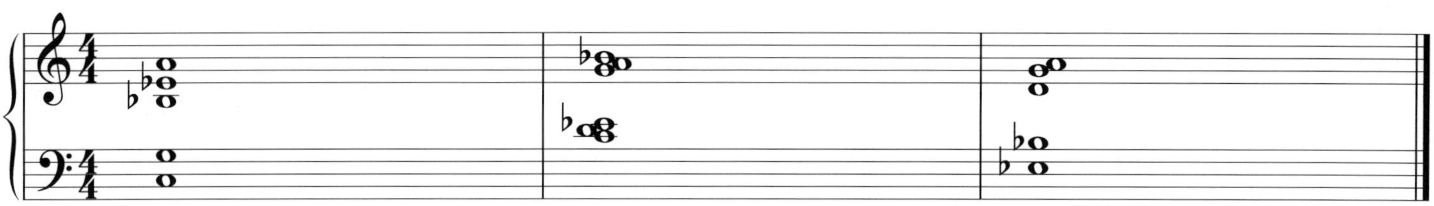

Group D: Technical Studies

In the assessment you will be asked to perform your choice of one of the following three technical studies along with the accompanying backing track.

Example 1 | Blues/Gospel – chordal comping study

Example 2 | Jazz – lydian dominant modal study

Example 3 | Action game soundtrack – locrian modal study

Sight Reading

In the assessment, you have a choice between either a Sight Reading test or an Improvisation & Interpretation test. The assessor will ask you which one you wish to choose before commencing. Once you have decided you cannot change your mind.

In the sight reading test, the assessor will give you a 12–16 measure melody in the key of either G♭ major or F♯ major. You will first be given 90 seconds to practise, after which the assessor will play the backing track twice. The first time is for you to practise and the second time is for you to perform the final version for the assessment. For each playthrough, the backing track will begin with a one measure count-in. The tempo is ♩=60–130.

During the practice time, you will be given the choice of a metronome click throughout or a one measure count in at the beginning.

The backing track is continuous, so once the first playthrough has finished, the count in of the second playing will start immediately.

Sight Reading | Example 1

Please note: The test shown is an example. The assessor will give you a different version in the assessment.

Sight Reading | Example 2

Please note: The test shown is an example. The assessor will give you a different version in the assessment.

Improvisation & Interpretation

In the assessment, you have a choice between either a Sight Reading test or an Improvisation & Interpretation test. The assessor will ask you which one you wish to choose before commencing. Once you have decided you cannot change your mind.

In the Improvisation & Interpretation test, the assessor will give you a 12–16 measure chord progression in the key of either F♯ major or G♭ major. You will first be given 90 seconds to practise, after which the assessor will play the backing track twice. The first time is for you to practise and the second time is for you to perform the final version for the assessment. For each playthrough, the backing track will begin with a one measure count-in. The tempo is ♩=60–130.

During the practice time, you will be given the choice of a metronome click throughout or a one measure count-in at the beginning.

The backing track is continuous, so once the first playthrough has finished, the count-in of the second playing will start immediately.

You will need to improvise melodies and chordal comping between left hand and right hand, in any way you wish, interpreting the chord progression and backing track given to you in the assessment.

Improvisation & Interpretation | Example 1

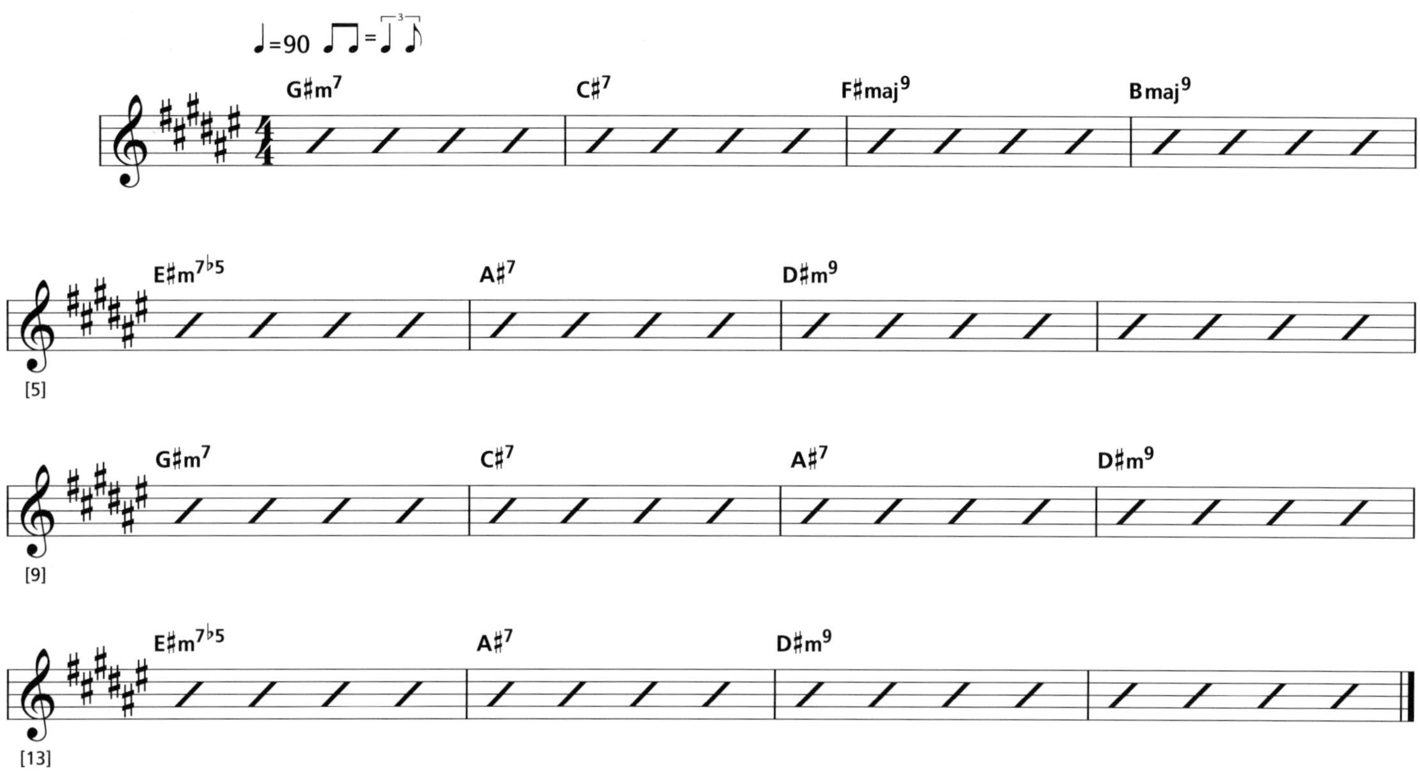

Please note: The test shown is an example: The assessor will give you a different version in the assessment

Improvisation & Interpretation | Example 2

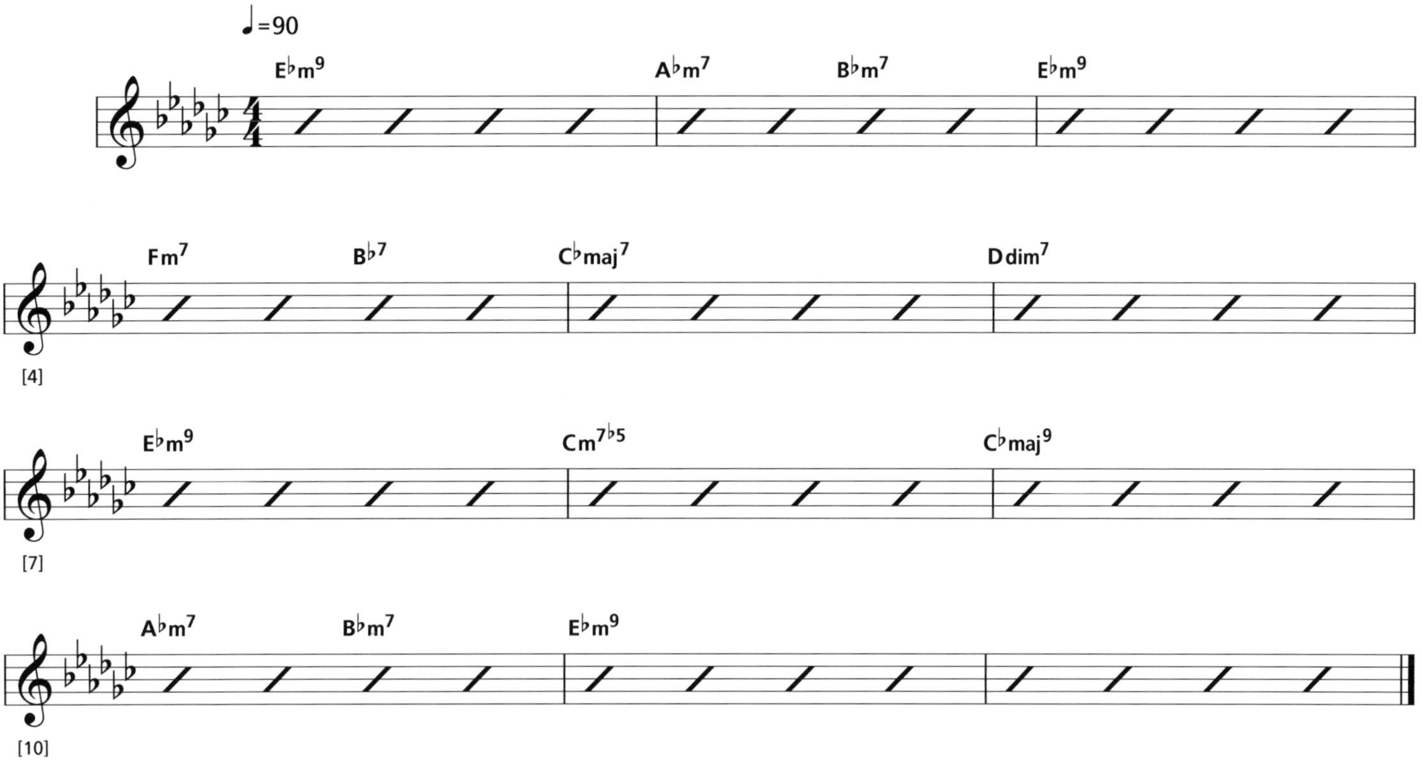

Please note: The test shown is an example: The assessor will give you a different version in the assessment

Ear Tests

In this section, there are two ear tests:

- Melodic Recall
- Harmonic Recall

You will find one example of each type of test printed below and you will need to perform both of them in the assessment.

Test 1: Melodic Recall

The assessor will play you a two measure diatonic melody in the key of C major with a range up to an octave. The first note will be the root note or the 5th. You will hear the test twice, each time with a one measure count-in, then you will hear a further one measure count-in after which you will need to play the melody to the click. The tempo is ♩= 95 bpm.

It is acceptable to play over the track as it is being played as well as practising after the second playthough. The length of time available after the second playthrough is pre-recorded on the audio track so the count-in may begin while you are still practising.

Please note: The test shown is an example. The assessor will give you a different version in the assessment.

Test 2: Harmonic Recall

The assessor will play you a chord progression containing chords I, II, III, IV, V, VI in any order or combination in the key of C major. You will hear the chord progression twice, each time with a one measure count-in. You will then hear a further one measure count in before playing back to a click. At this level/grade, seventh chords are introduced. Please note, there is no requirement for the chords to be voicing-specific. The tempo is ♩= 95 bpm.

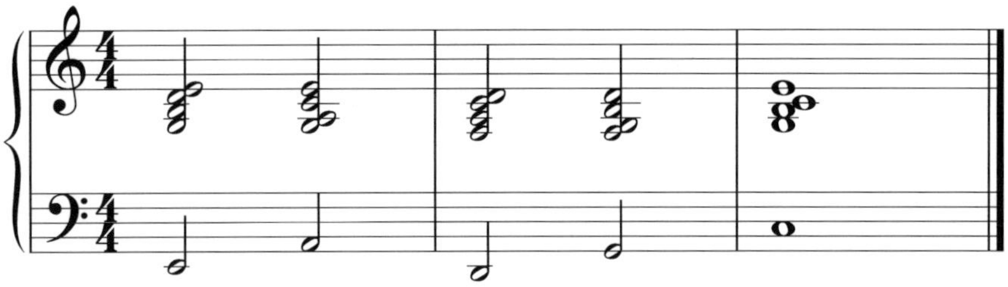

Please note: The test shown is an example. The assessor will give you a different version in the assessment.

General Musicianship Questions

The final part of your assessment is the General Musicianship Questions section, which features five questions relating to one of your choice of the performance pieces.

1. You will be asked a question relating to the harmony from a section of one of your pieces
2. You will be asked a question relating to the melody in a section of one of your pieces
3. You will be asked a question relating to the rhythms used in a section of one of your pieces
4. You will be asked a question relating to the technical requirements of one of your pieces
5. You will be asked a question relating to the genre of one of your pieces

Further guidance on the types of questions asked at this level/grade can be found at the RSL website *www.rslawards.com*

Entering Rockschool Assessments

Entering a Rockschool assessment is easy, just go online and follow our simple six step process. All details for entering online, dates, fees, regulations and Free Choice pieces can be found at *www.rslawards.com*

- All candidates should ensure they bring their own Level/Grade syllabus book to the assessment or have proof of digital purchase ready to show the assessor.

- All Level/Grade 6–8 candidates must ensure that they bring valid photo ID to their assessment.

Marking Schemes

Debut to Level/Grade 8

ELEMENT	PASS	MERIT	DISTINCTION
Performance Piece 1	12–14 out of 20	15–17 out of 20	18+ out of 20
Performance Piece 2	12–14 out of 20	15–17 out of 20	18+ out of 20
Performance Piece 3	12–14 out of 20	15–17 out of 20	18+ out of 20
Technical Exercises	9–10 out of 15	11–12 out of 15	13+ out of 15
Sight Reading *or* Improvisation & Interpretation	6 out of 10	7–8 out of 10	9+ out of 10
Ear Tests	6 out of 10	7–8 out of 10	9+ out of 10
General Musicianship Questions	3 out of 5	4 out of 5	5 out of 5
TOTAL MARKS	**60%+**	**74%+**	**90%+**

Performance Certificates | Debut to Level/Grade 8

ELEMENT	PASS	MERIT	DISTINCTION
Performance Piece 1	12–14 out of 20	15–17 out of 20	18+ out of 20
Performance Piece 2	12–14 out of 20	15–17 out of 20	18+ out of 20
Performance Piece 3	12–14 out of 20	15–17 out of 20	18+ out of 20
Performance Piece 4	12–14 out of 20	15–17 out of 20	18+ out of 20
Performance Piece 5	12–14 out of 20	15–17 out of 20	18+ out of 20
TOTAL MARKS	**60%+**	**75%+**	**90%+**

Copyright Information

Defying Gravity (from "Wicked")
(Schwartz)
Rodgers & Hammerstein Theatrical Europe Limited.

Africa
(Porcaro/Paich)
Sony/ATV Music Publishing/Kobalt Music Publishing Limited

Cantaloupe Island
(Hancock)
Kobalt Music Publishing Limited

He's A Pirate (from "Pirates Of The Caribbean: The Curse Of The Black Pearl")
(Zimmer/Badelt/Zanelli)
Universal Music Publishing Limited

In The End
(Bennington/Shinoda/Bourdon/Hahn/Delson)
Concord Music Publishing LLC

The Way It Is
(Hornsby)
Sony/ATV Music Publishing (UK) Limited

mcps

Piano Notation Explained

THE MUSICAL STAVE shows pitches and rhythms and is divided by lines into measures. Pitches are named after the first seven letters of the alphabet.

Grace Note: Play the grace note on or before the beat depending on the style of music, then move quickly to the note it leads onto.

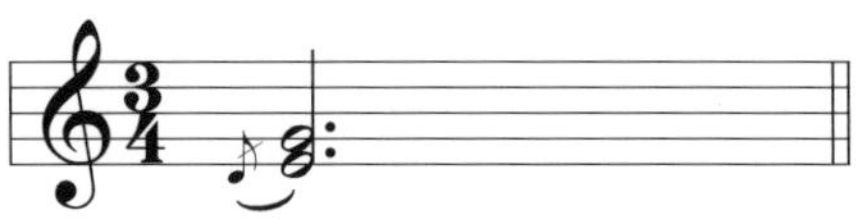

Pedal Marking: Depress and then release the sustain pedal. Multiple pedal operations in a short space of time may be simplified as shown in the last two beats of the measure below.

Spread Chord: Play the chord from the bottom note up (top down only if there is a downward arrow head). The final note should sound by the appropriate notated measure position.

Glissando: Play the notes between the notated pitches by sliding over the keyboard with the fingers or fingernails.

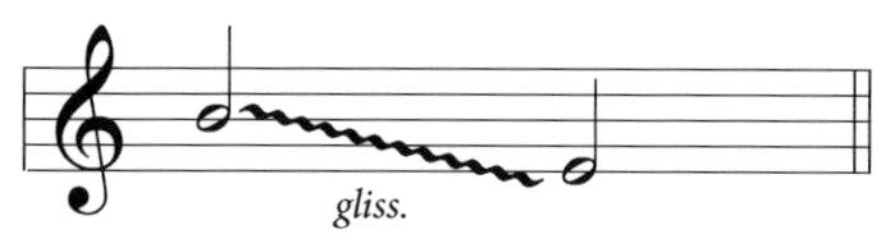

Tremolando: Oscillate at speed between marked notes.

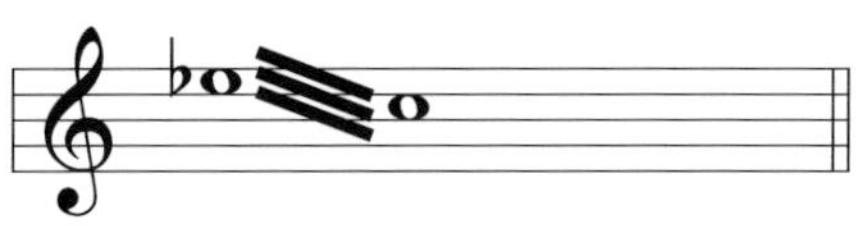

Finger Markings: These numbers represent your fingers. 1 is the thumb, 2 the index finger and so on.

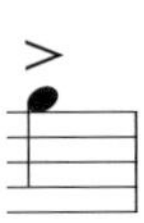 (accent) • Accentuate note (play it louder).

 (accent) • Accentuate note with great intensity.

 (staccato) • Shorten time value of note.

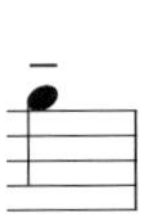 (accent) • Accentuate note with more arm weight.

D.𝄋. al Coda • Go back to the sign (𝄋), then play until the measure marked ***To Coda*** 𝄌 then skip to the section marked 𝄌 ***Coda***.

D.C. al Fine • Go back to the beginning of the song and play until the measure marked ***Fine*** (end).

Una Corda • Use soft pedal

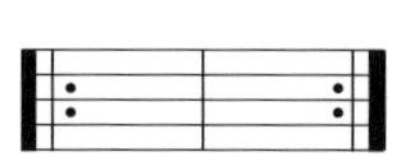 • Repeat the measures between the repeat signs.

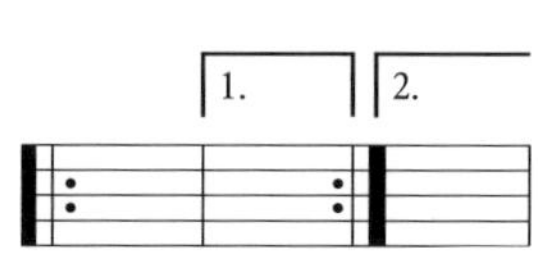

• When a repeated section has different endings, play the first ending only the first time and the second ending only the second time.